MS. BAROSS goes to
MEXICO
San Miguel de Allende

written and illustrated by Jan Baross

MPolo Press
Portland, Oregon

Cover and interior design by Jodi McPhee-Giddings
Edited by Lilia Trápaga Tenney, Stevan Allred, and Billie Green

Text set in Adobe Caslon
Display set in Nueva Standard and Adobe Caslon

MPolo Press
Publishers of award winning books

ISBN 978-0-9855303-9-6

Books by Jan Baross available at Amazon and all e-books:

Fiction: "Jose Builds a Woman"
Winner of Kay Snow Award for Fiction

Non-fiction: Travel: "Ms. Baross Goes to Paris"
"Ms. Baross Goes to Mexico: San Miguel de Allende"

Website: janbaross.com
Email: bmi@easystreet.net

To my mother, Estelle Meadoff, who opened my eyes to the world of travel.

Introduction

I never feel freer or happier than when I escape the chill of Oregon's winter into the warm Mexican countryside. For five months I live in the colonial village of San Miguel de Allende where the flow of life is gentler and simpler. The colors are powerful enough to inhale.

This graphic diary represents thirty years of sketching San Miguel and its people. The style, rhythm and line of the drawings have changed with the passing decades. But San Miguel remains timeless in a country that inspires my imagination like no other.

—Jan Baross, 2013

December

After a stop over in Houston, we land in the sunny Benito Juarez Airport. The 70 degree heat and warm light makes me feel ten years younger. Nights can be chilly but I've got my Oregon layers to keep me warm.

Travelers tip: *The best weather is March. The least expensive route to San Miguel is through Mexico City. The more expensive and convenient flights land in Querétaro (QRO) about 45 miles away from San Miguel, or Leon-Guanajuato-Aero Puerto del Bajio (BJX) airport about 70 miles away. Shuttle reservations to San Miguel: Bajio or Viaje. They can be late. If they don't show up, you have an expensive taxi ride. But, so far, I've had no problem.*

www.experience-san-miguel-de-allende.com is a good site for detailed maneuvering around San Miguel.

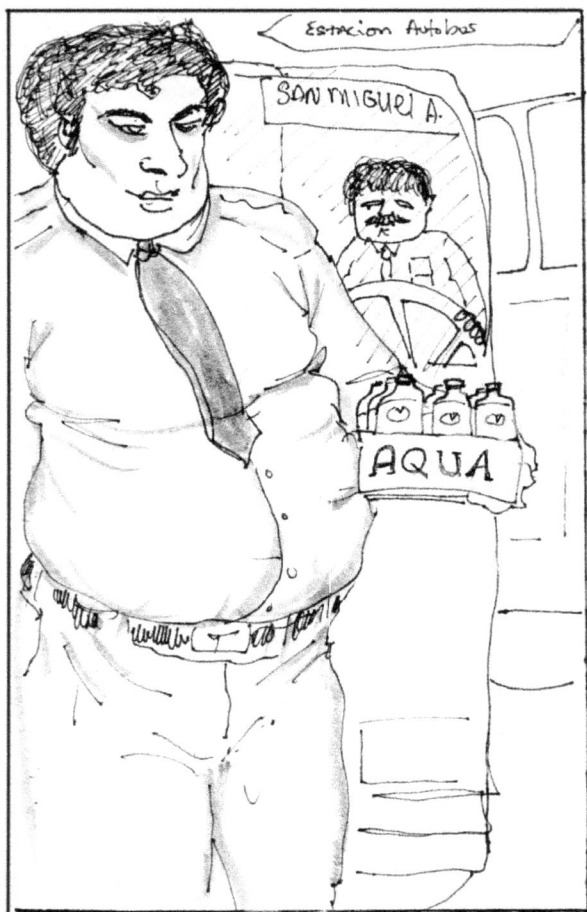

Mexico City Airport

I run the gauntlet of customs and head for the first class buses at the airport that will take me to San Miguel de Allende.

Travelers tip: *ETN and Primera Plus, are the directo, express. If you stay in Mexico City the www.hotelgillow.com or www.hotelcatedral.com are good locations. Your hotel will order you a safe taxi to the Autobus Estación Terminal Norte for San Miguel.*

Bus to San Miguel de Allende

Years ago I traveled on second-class buses from Mexico City to San Miguel. Animals were allowed. Windows didn't shut. Newspapers and candy wrappers flew around my head like kites. Today first class has air-conditioning, a free lunch, reclining seats and small TV monitors with American flicks or black and white Mexican movies. It's a four hour drive northwest past towns, markets and farms into the Guanajuato mountains that rise over six thousand feet.

Oratorio de San Felipe Neri
Calle Independencia

Arriving in San Miguel I feel like I'm home. My first purchase is a big bottle of water. Dehydration is a suck on the system with this altitude and heat. The taxi ride (two to three dollars) to my rented casita reacquaints me with the hilly town. It was founded in 1542 by a Franciscan monk, Fray Juan de San Miguel. The town eventually became the market center for surrounding haciendas trading in cattle and textiles. It was also a stop over for a booming

silver trade. The ruling Spanish class built opulent churches and mansions that are the eye candy of San Miguel.

Traveler tip: *About a mile or so from the center of San Miguel by taxi is the restored chapel of founder Fray Juan de San Miguel. The area is called San Miguel de Viejo.*

Captain Ignacio Allende
Independencia Square

The man on the horse is the town hero. In 1810, Ignacio Allende of San Miguel, a captain in the Spanish army, teamed up with a renegade Mexican priest, Father Hidalgo, from the neighboring town of Dolores Hidalgo. They planned an uprising against the wealthy Spanish. It failed and the men were executed. But their courageous effort led to the Mexican War of Independence. Allende was added to the town's name in 1826.

Restoration in San Miguel

San Miguel was almost a ghost town by 1926, with only a third of the population remaining. Depleted silver mines, the War of Independence from Spain (1810-1821) and the Mexican Revolution (1910-1921) all took their toll. The crumbling town was declared a national historic monument by the Mexican government. The colonial buildings were restored and today there are over eighty thousand people living in San Miguel. As a UNESCO World Heritage site, San Miguel benefits from an on going, mildly subsidized facelift. This includes tearing up cobblestone streets to put wires underground and then replacing the stones.

Art Colony

Foreigners started arriving after World War Two on the G.I. Bill and enrolled in San Miguel's art and language schools. Today there's a permanent community of around ten thousand international expatriates, many of them artists and writers. People enjoy living here because it's cheaper, beautiful, the crime rate is low, but most of all there is a welcoming, social lifestyle.

Casita

I settle into my casita and take a moment on the roof garden for big *hola* to San Miguel. I never get tired of the view, yellows, reds and earth browns, the classic colors of the colonial period. Hazy mountains surround the town and in the distance are the pink spires of the Parroquia. I grab my sun-proof hat and buzz down to the Jardín (main square) to see which of my snowbird buddies have arrived.

Sidewalks of San Miguel

The cobblestone streets are preserved as they were 400 years ago. The Mexicans call the sidewalks anti-romantico because they are so narrow couples can't walk hip to hip. Imbued as I am with American speed, I step off the narrow sidewalk in order to pass the Mexicans. It always takes me time to get into their slower pace. Last year I was thrilled when a Mexican actually passed me. On the way to the Jardín, I notice the broad smiles on everyone's faces. People seem happier here. Ex-pat pals tell me that in San Miguel they have become more the persons they always hoped to be. I wonder if it takes another culture to release the best in some of us.

Parroquia de San Miguel Arcangel

Every time I enter the Jardín, I'm enchanted all over again. The towering pink sandstone church, a Neo-Gothic parish, is San Miguel's emblematic heart. It was built in the late 17th century in a plain Franciscan style. In 1880, a stone carver and mason, Zeferino Gutiérrez, re-designed the façade from a postcard of a European Gothic cathedral giving it his own Mexican spin. Some call it Disney Gothic. There is delicacy and strength in the ornate stones that change color in the shifting light. The original church bell, cast in 1732, begins ringing in the early morning and seems to have no connection to mortal time.

Mexican Weddings

What is the sound of 100 *I do's*? In the Parroquia hundreds of couples can be married simultaneously. Mexicans are all about family, and this becomes a shared familial event. One gigantic ceremony is also easier on the

pocketbook. After the wedding couples flow out of the giant wooden doors. Brides look like floating gardens. Small children throw flower petals and horse carriages arrive for the couples as Mariachis play.

The Jardín

In front of the Parroquia, foot traffic centers around an iron-grilled bandstand. The laurel trees are trimmed round like a bowl haircut. There used to be hundreds of grackles chirping above our heads so loudly that we had to shout to be heard. The local government eliminated the nests, but the

Jardin is still people-noisy. Conversations usually begin with, "Where are you from?" In one afternoon I met a Bulgarian businesswoman, a Malaysian poet, a painter from Uzbekistan. No need for intricate social plans. Just meet up in the Jardín, gather on the uncomfortable iron benches and decide where to go.

Mariachis

As the sun sets, Mariachi bands saunter into the Jardín tuning their
instruments. They dress in tight black or white pants with metal buttons
down the sides and short jackets to match. It gets interesting when several
bands are hired at the same time by different people to play different songs

in different parts of the Jardín, a mildly discordant form of Mexican torture. Campo bands play dance tunes on the weekends. I especially like the older Mexican couples who seem to have been dancing together all their lives. It's like watching a private conversation.

Indian Conchero Dancers in the Jardín

On different holidays Indian men, women and children in peacock feathers
and beautiful traditional costumes dance all day in the hot sun. They bang

cowhide drums and shake rattles while surrounded by the modern world of
taxis, cell phones and cameras. Naturally, I sit in the shade of the arcade, sip
water and watch them re-create their ancient spectacle of cosmic motion.

Promenade in the Jardín

When I first came to San Miguel in the 80s I looked forward to the traditional weekend promenade. It no longer exists, but it was fun to watch parental chaperones keeping an eye on their hormonal teens. As the band played, boys circled in one direction flirting with the girls coming toward them from the opposite direction. As the youngsters passed each other, they flirted *yes* with shy smiles while parental faces reflected a resounding, *no*. Mating rituals have modernized, even in San Miguel. Now the kids meet in the Jardín and cling to each other like Velcro. Is it a sign of growing older that I prefer the good old days of the innocent promenade?

The Noises of San Miguel

Day or night, Mexico is loud. Church bells ring, carousel music announces a bottled water truck is coming, the knife sharpener rings his bicycle bell, vendors echo their wares through the streets, a man clangs two pieces of metal together warning that the garbage pick-up is on its way. Add Indian drums, dogs, mariachis, firecrackers exploding all night, roosters in the morning, and it gets pretty intense. Still, I'm happy to trade my quiet life in the U.S. for this unpredictable symphony.

Shoeshine

On each corner of the Jardín is a shoeshine stand. Behold, the shiner and the shinee. Getting my own battered walking shoes bathed in suds and color once a week is a sensual little break in the day. It's also a chance to people-watch and sketch the lived-in faces.

Chiclet Kids

If you sit in the Jardín for very long, the Chiclet kids descend. I buy their gum to help out, but the sweet taste makes my teeth curl.

Mounted Police

Since there are no disturbances to subdue in the Jardín, the main duty of the mounted policemen seems to be giving directions to tourists. Their eighteenth century garb helps to sustain the illusion of a more romantic time.

Ice Cream Horse

The most beloved animal in the Jardín is the ice cream horse, a huge Clydesdale that pulls a red wooden ice cream wagon. The horse stands patiently as tourists climb on his back for photos. That horse has had his picture taken so many times he probably thinks he's famous.

Dogs of San Miguel

Hundreds of dogs used to roam around town. Some were real characters. 'Lupita the Bar Dog' was famous for keeping the late night drinkers company. When she got ill, there were collection boxes in the bars to pay for her treatment. Now there are leash laws and spaying. It's a nostalgic blast from the past to see a feral pooch running free. There's always the growling roof dogs pacing their small territory above our heads.

Atencíon News

The *Atencíon* bilingual weekly is sold in the Jardin by a big-bellied vendor. The paper lists coming attractions. Check out the historic walking and bus tours. The Homes of San Miguel Tour can be a stunning revelation in wealth and taste.

Biblioteca Pública
Calle Insurgentes #25

The Biblioteca Pública is one of the centers of San Miguel's cultural ecosystem. The library was begun by Helen Wale, a Canadian who had a collection of children's books in her home. It has become the largest privately funded, publicly accessible library in Mexico, with the second largest collection of English language books. There's a small store near the

entrance that sells works of local authors and artist. Through an archway the Santa Ana Café is a welcome retreat for enjoying nibbles and reading a book in the shade of an expansive Jacaranda.

Traveler tip: *Purchase a library card and the stacks are yours. If the door to the Quetzal Room is open take a look at the colorful, stylized mural by a local artist David Leonardo.*

THEATRES OF SAN MIGUEL

Santa Ana Theater in the Biblioteca Pública

Another aspect of the library is the Santa Ana Theater for plays, films and lectures. The ticket office and entrance are right off the Santa Ana Café. One of my favorite performances was the Collar de Viento Band, Huitchol Indians from the Northern states of Nayarit and San Luis Potosí. The band played ancient instruments that sounded like the wind. Huicholes are famous for their peyote ceremonies, for yarn paintings depicting their myths and visions, and for their minute beadwork. In a Mexico City art museum I once saw an entire Volkswagen covered in their beads of intricate design.

Teatro Ángela Peralta
Corner of Calle Hernández Macias/Mesones

Teatro Ángela Peralta is the largest and oldest theater in San Miguel. It opened in 1873 as an opera house with a performance by the soprano Angela Peralta. Over the decades international artists have enriched our evenings with a wealth of eclectic entertainment.

Local Thespians

For such a small town, I found a lot of theater groups when I was casting my play, "Mata Hari." Of the groups that still exist, the oldest is Player's Workshop. They raised money to build the Santa Ana Theater. The Play Readers, Sindicato, Shakespeare Readers and El Caldero have been around forever. Shelter Theater is more recent. El Totopo and La Comedia del Universo are for kids. The satirical Literary Cabaret has had an enthusiastic following for decades.

Bullring

I entered the gates of the bullring to see a famous matador, but I fell in love with the bull. He ran out snorting, fierce and indomitable. He charged again and again in spite of his wounds. By the end, he'd been reduced to a bleeding, slump-shouldered animal on shaky legs. His eyes looked bewildered. He'd gone from peak virility to infirmity in less than an hour. I left as the bull's dead body was chained to two burros and dragged from the ring. At least, they tell you, the poor will eat well tonight.

Instituto Allende Art School
Calle Ancha San Antonio #20

Stirling Dickinson, a writer and artist, arrived in 1938. He made his home in a former tannery, raised orchids and rode a burro. In the 40s, he was one of the men most instrumental in transforming the little village of San Miguel into an international center for artists by establishing Instituto Allende in the

former home of the wealthy Canal family. The art and language classrooms, galleries and cafes are all built around beautiful plazas.

Traveler tip: *For a list of the many art galleries, shops, restaurants see the tourist office near Hotel San Francisco, the kiosk in the main square and the web.*

Bellas Artes
Calle Dr. Hernández Macias #75

Co-founded by Stirling Dickinson, the Centro Cultural Bellas Artes has been an international art school since the 40s. The building was a beautiful two-story, mid-18th century convent. It's been restructured into classrooms, huge galleries with a David Alfaro Siqueiros mural and a theater upstairs for lectures. The classes are so popular I haven't gotten into one yet. It's also one of the few islands of serenity in noisy San Miguel. I like to sit in the small café under shaded arches, sip coffee and allow myself to be lulled by cooing pigeons flapping in the sunlit spray of an enormous fountain.

Fabrica Aurora
Calzada de la Aurora, Colonia Aurora

This former turn-of-the-century textile mill has become a huge mall of art galleries and small wonderful cafes. Every month new shows open with a gala celebration of food, wine, music and people in their dress-up best. I like to go when the galleries are silent and I can absorb the new work.

ARTY SIDE TRIPS

Galería Atotonilco
www.folkartsanmiguel.com

Fifteen minutes from town by taxi is the enormous modern home and gallery of Mayer Shacter and his wife Susan Page. The art gallery and home are filled with Mayer's collection of Mexican crafts. He has great stories to tell about his unique works of art. Buy or browse, it's worth the trip.

Anado McLauchlin
www.madebyanado.com

Artist Anado McLauchlin and his partner Richard live in an imaginative home of inlaid altars, tiles, sculptures, color and fabric. Next to the home is the Chapel of Jimmy Ray, another wonderfully sensual overload. Mosaics and colored bottles are embedded in concrete walls that stretch up to a vaulted ceiling. Anado's wild imagination is from the heart of the unleashed 60s. A trip to his home is a real trip.

SAN MIGUEL SHOPS

San Miguel Shoes / Zapatería Martha
Relox #30 www.milagrosparati.com

There are wonderful shops all over town. I'll mention two that I find entertaining. Doña Martha, the Mexican doyenne of an international shoe empire, sits in her store reading a huge Bible. She dresses in brightly colored suits, matching shoes and a wide-brimmed hat that practically hides her face. She'll answer shoe questions and then it's back to the good book.

Casa Cohen Relox #16, Centro
One half block from the Jardín

The Cohen family's hardware store opened in the early 1900s. The Cohens were the first Jewish residents in the now extensive San Miguel Jewish community. They emigrated from Aleppo, Syria. The father had a dream of animals, which transmuted into gargoyles on the building's façade along with Jewish stars.

CAFES AND RESTAURANTS

Café del Jardín
Corner of the Jardín/Umarán

An old timer told me that when the going gets tough, Mexicans open a restaurant. Perhaps that is why there are so many good eateries. The ones I frequent are not likely to disappear before you get there. But if they're gone that's because, as people say, *this is Mexico*, and that is the sensible philosophical response to most things that happen here. The Café del Jardin is where I prefer my morning coffee and paper because I enjoy watching the flower vendors set up under the arches as the sun spread slowly over the Parroquia's pink stones. Occasionally the colorful hot air balloon ride drifts overhead.

Starbucks
Canal #3

Originally there were demonstrations against Starbucks by both Mexicans and gringos. They wanted to insure that if the coffee giant moved in, San Miguel's colonial style would be preserved. As a result, the town has a handsome colonial Starbucks with outdoor garden seating.

El Correo
Correo #23

My old haunt, across from the Post Office. Great Aztec soup and good Mexican food. Around the corner is **El Pegaso**, *Corregidora #6*. It's also been around for decades. Good food and waiters with personality. I like their chicken soup. **Mama Mia's,** *Calle Umarán #8*. Covered patio. I always order enchiladas verdes. Music in the evenings. Next door is **Pueblo Viejo,** *Calle Umarán #6*. Upstairs bar for margaritas and a sunset view. **Café Berlin,** *Umarán #19* is a gringo hang out, good art and food. **La Posadita**, *Calle Cuna de Allende #13*. It's great for dinner and a romantic view of the Parroquia. Close by, **El Ten Ten Pie,** *corner of Calle Cuna de Allende #21 /Cuadrante*. It's a popular outdoor hangout.

Café de la Parroquia
Calle Jesus #11

A block off the Jardín. Good food, an outdoor patio around a flower-laden fountain. **La Crepe**, *Calle Hospicio* #37. My favorite, a Mediterranean atmosphere. They serve crepes and tasty salads. Yes, I eat the salads. **Vivoli**, *Hernandez Macias* #66, is good for Italian fair. Up the street is **Bezzito Restaurant and Lounge**, #78 *Hernández Macias*. This hip restaurant has an illuminated waterfall and a roof bar with a stream running through. **Hank's New Orleans Café and Oyster Bar**, *Hildago* #12 . Party atmosphere and good food. They celebrate Carnival/Mardi Gras with giant paper maché puppets called Mojigangas.

Rosewood Hotel
Calle Nemesio Diez #11
SanMiguel@rosewoodhotels.com

Total luxury hotel and restaurant with amazing pool facilities. It caters to the rich but I go anyway. Their Luna Rooftop Tapas Bar is open to the skies with large booths and has one of the grander views of San Miguel, especially at sunset. Not far is **Hecho en México,** *Ancha San Antonio* #8. This is one of the best places for lunch or dinner with large American helpings and consistently good food.

Café Etc.
Relox #37

Across from the Biblioteca Pública. Gringos call it Juan's, after the owner.
The food is always good. You can purchase quality bulk coffee and read the
English magazines. Close by is **Café Muro,** *Calle Loreto* #10B. Another of
my favorites. Geraldo and Carlos are the friendly owners of this bright
red café with an eclectic art gallery. Breakfast and lunches are beautifully
crafted. **Olé Olé Restaurant,** *Calle Loreto* #66. Walls covered in bullfight
memorabilia. Love their arrachera (flank steak).

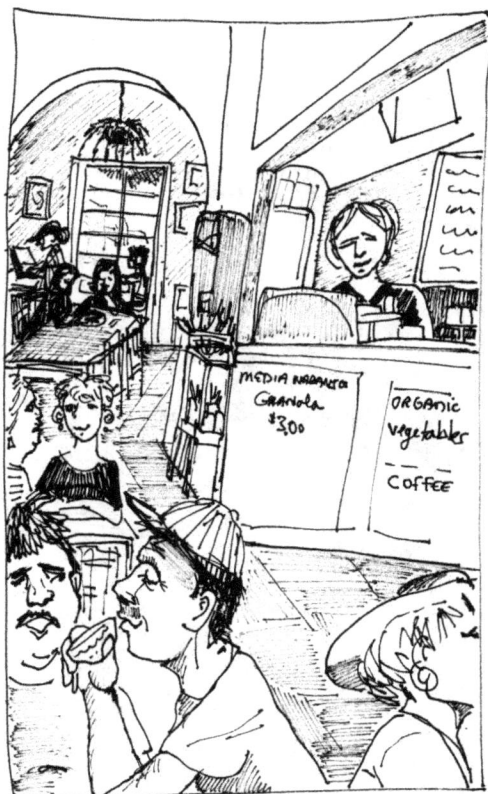

Media Naranja Restaurant
Hidalgo #83 / La Luz

A small popular upstairs café run by Rodrigo Sautto and his wife. Organic food, free wifi and a small book exchange. **Vía Orgánica Cafe,** *Calle Margarito Ledesma #2,* is in the Colonia Guadalupe barrio (neighborhood). Good organic food, outdoor dining and an organic grocery store with specialty items.

☞ **Traveler tips:** *Near Vía Ogánica is El Pato, Margarito Ledesma #19, the town's best art supply shop. Most of Colonia Guadalupe's street signs are named after Mexican songs or songwriters, like Calle Cri Cri, a famous children's composer.*

Tio Lucas Restaurant and Bar
Calle Mesones, #103.

Tio Lucas is a popular jazz restaurant run by Max. He's good looking and the food is even better. **Socialita Restaurant**, *Correo* #45. I usually have my birthday bash here. High-end but worth it. **Chamonix Restaurant**, *Sollano* #17, serene courtyard, great indoor service. Asian and French inspired cuisine. Consistently excellent. **Mesones de San Jose**, #80 *Mesones*, a long archway takes you to a tree shaded patio. It's an historic setting and very pleasant for breakfast and lunch. Cash only.

BAKERIES

The Blue Door Bakery
Relox #21

The Blue Door has a plaque on the door that reads "Panderia La Colemena 1901-2001." **La Buena Vida Bakery,** *Calle Hernández Macías* #72, is in back of Café Contento. Across from the Belles Artes, both the bakery and the café are good quality. The café often has a lecture series. **Petit Four,** *Mesones* #99 is great for a rich chocolate fix.

VENDORS

Food Carts

Food carts in the Jardin had always been a part of the landscape. But now, they are a thing of the past. Follow your nose to the side streets for fried meat stands and hot corn slathered in warm questionable mayonnaise.

Moveable Feasts

Wheeling vendors are selling throughout the town. They have a sharp marketing tool: their voice. It cuts through the sounds of traffic. Peanuts! Corn! Garlic! Cacahuate! Maiz! Ajo! Actually it sounds more appealing in Spanish.

Fresh Vegetable Vendors

These women are selling cut-up nopal cactus amid the fumes of a popular bus stop on Insurgentes.

My Favorite Vendor

In the sun, the balloons look like a neon colored bouquet above his head. I'd like to see a strong wind scoop him up past the spires of the Parroquia. A Mexican Mary Poppins moment.

Mexican Insulation

Wool snakes are a necessity to stop the drafts under doors.

Firewood Vendor

One of the things I'm happy *not* to see anymore are old women carrying bundles of firewood to sell.

Burros

Burros not only carry firewood. Their heavy bags are full of rich lakeside topsoil for gringo gardens. March is the annual burro race fundraiser in nearby Jalapa where the little beasts have a frolic day and are decorated in colorful crepe.

MARKETS OF SAN MIGUEL

Mercado Ignacio Ramírez
Calle Colegio/one block north of Calle Mesones

This is the largest traditional covered market in town. Inside a warehouse-sized building are produce, meat, flowers, clothes, restaurants and much more. Outside is the **Artisan's Market.** It winds down a long staircase to the next street on Calle Loreto. I always buy bright red earrings made from dyed Jacaranda seeds. I can't tell you how many compliments I get. **Tuesday Market** is a bus or taxi ride up to the mesa above town. Ask the bus driver where to get off. You'll see the giant tents. It's a shopper's paradise for high and low end. Be prepared to sift. For regular groceries, I shop at **Bonanza,** *Mesones* #37.

HOTELS OF SAN MIGUEL

Hotel Sautto
Hernández Macias #59

As a budget traveler, I'll name a couple of places where I've stayed over the years. Hotel Sautto went for $10 a room in the 80s. It was a convent with thick walls, no heating, orange trees, loud parrots, and a restaurant. It has an excellent location and is still relatively easy on the wallet. **Hotel Posada de las Monjas,** (*house of nuns*) *Canal* #37. I stayed there for three winters. This too was a convent. It's not hard to pretend you're doing penance in this warren of cement rooms with a cross over each bed. Their restaurant serves cafeteria quality food and has a beautiful view of the mountains from the third floor terrace.

Casa de los Soles
Loreto #19
www.casadelossoles.com

Finally I could afford this small hotel run by a patient Mexican couple. Jorge and Sandra Garcidueñas will let you practice your Spanish on them. It's a great location because the artisan market is next door, the food market is close and the library is down the street. You enter through an Internet

shop into the courtyard of the three-story hotel. The courtyard walls are completely covered with brightly painted suns. The apartments are clean and you can ask for an electric heater.

👉 **Traveler tip**: *There are many good hotels and B&Bs on the web. I rent casitas now on VRBO and other websites. Check to make sure your hotel is not located on one of the steep hills unless you don't mind hiking.*

MUSEUMS OF SAN MIGUEL

Mask Museum
Cuesta de San Jose #32

I used to collect masks so I enjoy this private collection. There are over **400** masks on display, and video documentaries of indigenous ceremonies. **Museo Histórico de San Miguel de Allende**, *Calle Cuna de Allende* #1, on the corner of the Jardín. This was where Ignacio Allende's family lived and where he was born. **Museo in Casa Mayorazgo de La Canal**, *Hidalgo/Canal*. The front door of the former Canal family is carved in a beautiful neo-classical style. Behind the door is the Casa de Cultura de Banamex which exhibits the region's history. **Toy Museum** "La Esquina," *corner of Nunez/ SanFrancisco*. This is fun and not just for kids. There are over a thousand well-crafted Mexican folk toys on display.

LANGUAGE SCHOOLS

Warren Hardy Spanish
San Rafael #6
www.warrenhardy.com

There are so many good language schools in San Miguel it's hard to choose. I liked Warren's method. He's a charismatic teacher who, along with his wife Tuli, has turned his language program into an international enterprise.

PARKS AND GARDENS OF SAN MIGUEL

El Charco del Ingenio Botanical Gardens

On a dry mesa above San Miguel is a one hundred and sixty-seven acre preserve, with a reservoir and small man-made islands for wild life. Begun in 1989 by a Mexican non-profit, it's one of the best botanical gardens in Mexico and an important center for research and conservation of cactus and succulents. There is a morning tour over the dusty trails to view cactus, spring fed pools, and a large greenhouse.

Music in the Botanical Garden

Every Solstice we gather in the garden's natural amphitheater of rocks and stone for musical performances that reverberate throughout the canyons.

Traveler tip: *Taxi up early before the heat kicks in. Just say "Botanica" and the taxi driver will know what you want. You can snack and buy water at their tiny cafe.*

Parque Juarez
Calle De Aldama / El Cardo

Parque Juarez was designed in the early 1900s with fountains and sculptures. It's situated on the bank of a river that's usually dry, but herons still build their nests in the lofty trees. It's a very family friendly place with a children's

playground, sun-dappled footpaths for strolls, benches for the grown ups, basketball leagues, artists displaying their work and all kinds of musical events.

WATERS OF SAN MIGUEL

El Paseo del Chorro
Above Parque Juarez

After Fray Juan de San Miguel founded the original town in 1542, his
successor, Fray Bernardo Cossin, moved the settlement to the natural
springs of El Chorro, the oldest neighborhood of San Miguel. The Indians

called the waters *Izcuinapan, place of the dogs.* According to legend, it was the dogs who led the men to water. In 1901 long rows of spring-fed, red cement basins were built for the women to do their wash.

☞ **Travelers tips:** *Above the red tubs of Chorro is a steep, winding pedestrian path to La Casa de Cultural where sometimes there are creative projects involving the locals.*

THERMAL HOT SPRINGS

La Gruta Hot Springs

This entire region is famous for hot springs. My favorite spa is La Gruta, a short **15** minute taxi or bus ride outside of town. La Gruta covers several grassy acres with three outdoor pools, a grotto and a small restaurant. In the old days, our gang would rent La Gruta for the night. After food, wine

and song we'd wobble down to the pools, change into swimsuits and wade into the hot starry water up to our chests. Candles held high, we paddled into a long dark tunnel where at the end there was a steamy cave. It was like entering a womb by candlelight. We took turns letting the hot waterfall pound our bodies limp.

Xote Hot Springs
Parque Acuatico

Xote Hot Springs have expansive gardens, several large hot pools, a giant water slide, shop, snacks, and a broad view of a valley. **Taboada Hot Springs** is one large fenced-in pool that is good for laps. It's set in the middle of dry acreage with no café. **Escondido Hot Springs** have nine water holes of

varying heat and you bring your own everything. In town we used to swim at **Pasada de Aldea Hotel** on *Calle Ancha de San Antonio* #15 for a small fee.

☛ **Traveler tip:** *All the hot springs are ten to fifteen minutes outside of town. Don't pay the taxi until he comes back to pick you up, or he may not return. If you take the bus, ask the driver where to get back on.*

Pharmacia
Calle Hernández Macías/Canal

I'll just mention pharmacies because you'll probably need one. The most famous pharmacy belongs to Consuelo (*nicknamed Chelo*). She is a small, sweet-faced grandmother and one of the wealthiest landowners in town. She speaks English and is the go-to gal for ailing gringos.

San Miguel is jokingly referred to as "the city of fallen women." Between inappropriate footwear, sidewalks with protruding metal, inexplicable potholes, unforgiving cobblestones and brittle bones, you see a number of people with casts and bruises. Forget about suing. In Mexico you are really on your own. But the doctors and hospitals are good. I had my broken wrist set at Hospital De Le Fe.

Traveler tip: *Hospital de Le Fe. Libramiento Jose Manuel Zavala.* 415-152-2233.

Charities: Casa Hogar Santa Julia

San Miguel is the land of fundraisers. Just about everyone is involved. I was impressed by the good works of the nuns at Casa Hogar Santa Julia Girl's Orphanage. Robin Loving and many volunteers help raise funds to support about forty girls and provide for their education, their medical needs and their future.

👉 **Traveler tip:** *Donations: www.santajulia.org*

San Miguel Writer's Conference

There are many conferences in San Miguel that I enjoy, but my favorite is the **San Miguel Writers Conference**. Begun in 2006 by Susan Page, Jody Fagan and hard working volunteers, it's grown into an international bi-lingual event. It attracts well-known authors such as Margaret Atwood, Barbara Kingsolver, Tom Robbins, Sandra Cisneros, Cheryl Strayed and Luis Urrea. What I like about the conference is the casual atmosphere. Everyone is accessible including the celebrated authors. Susan Page also began the monthly Literary Salon that invites local authors like myself to read from our new works.

MY FAVORITE MEXICAN HOLIDAYS

January: St Anthony's Day
The Blessing of the Animals

The plaza in front of the Oratorio Church fills with people dragging their pets to the priest. He stands on the stone steps and sprinkles water on the animals and sometimes their owners. Everyone looks spiffed up and beaming including the animals.

Traveler tip: *portalsanmiguel.com for a complete calendar of annual events.*

February: Candelaria-Spring

Candelaria is the unofficial beginning of spring in San Miguel. It's celebrated in Parque Juárez with farmers bringing their plants and seeds to sell. The park is turned into a huge colorful market with all kinds of plants that customers wheel out by the cartload.

March: El Señor de la Columna on Good Friday

Hundreds of people walk in the eight mile procession from the Sanctuary of Atotonilco, a world heritage site, to San Miguel. Leading the parade is a group of Mexican men carrying a wooden platform with the statue of Jesus called El Señor de la Columna. By early morning, exhausted and exalted, marchers enter San Miguel over chamomile strewn streets leaving a sweet

herbal smell to blend with the incense. They shuffle through brightly colored woodchip patterns and finally reach the church of San Juan de Dios. El Señor de la Columna and other holy statues are paraded into the Parroquia with locals playing Jesus, the disciples and musical Roman Centurions. On Wednesday of Easter Week El Senor del Columna is returned to the sanctuary of Atotonilco. This **400** year-old tradition is celebrated all over Mexico, but San Miguel is known for having the most elaborate pageantry.

March: Night of the Altars

One of the loveliest traditions is the Night of the Altars, on the Friday before Holy Week, the last Friday of Lent. It is a custom that began in the 1600s honoring La Virgen de Dolores (Our Lady of Sorrows). It is a very human to human honoring of a mother's suffering for her son's agony and death. Fountains symbolizing her tears are decorated with flowers, sweet and sour oranges, purple paper flags, and yellow wheat sprouts grown in the dark to represent her son's resurrection. Families build amazing altars

in their homes with carved holy figures that have been passed down for centuries. They invite the public in for traditional food and icies (cold drinks) to sooth the lump of sorrow in your throat.

Traveler tip: *Good streets for the visual feast: Calle Loreto, Calle Barranca, Peralta Theater, corner of Mesones/Hernandez Macias.*

March: Easter

The holy week of Easter is called Samana Santa. The Jardín is filled with people selling very special Easter eggs. The contents of the eggs have been cleaned out through a hole and the shell is filled with confetti and corn meal. The children run up and smash eggs over each other's head. I'm not sure what the significance is, but it's fun to buy a few eggs and chase the kids around the Jardín. Until they sneak up and smash eggs on my head. Nothing quite like that feeling of grit and confetti in my holiday hair.

March / April: Blowing Up Judas

After the solemn ceremonies and parades of holy week everyone is ready for a wow finish. One of the traditions is to hang paper maché figures of Judas over the street in the main square. As a climax to the holy week celebrations, the swaying bodies are blown to bits.

October: The Blessing of the Taxis

Hundreds of taxis decorated with flowers and balloons roll parade-fashion into the Jardín. The drivers park in front of the Parroquia and receive a blessing for their livelihoods.

November: Dia de los Muertos, Day of the Dead

Dia de los Muertos, with roots in Aztec culture, is celebrated in connection with All Saints Day. November 1st is for the infants who have passed and November 2nd is for the adults. At the cemeteries families place favorite foods and drinks of the loved one on the decorated grave. Sugar skulls, marigolds and figurines like the popular Catrina doll are some of the decorations used to honor the dead. The day has also become an excuse for a citywide costume party with everyone dressing up wildly and cheerfully muerto.

Homeward in April

The end always seems abrupt since time carries us so gently in Mexico. April winds are here and even the dust is hot on my skin. There were so many adventures and odd coincidences that could only have happened in San Miguel. I bid goodbye to friends old and new who have shared miles of talks and cobblestones walks. We say adios knowing next winter we will find each other again in the Jardín, and eat and drink together in the cafes of San Miguel.